Butterfly Gardening with Native Plants

How to Attract and Identify Butterflies

CHRISTOPHER KLINE

Skyhorse Publishing

Skyhorse Publishing books may be purchased in bulk at special discounts for sales promotion, corporate gifts, fund-raising, or educational purposes. Special editions can also be created to specifications. For details, contact the Special Sales Department, Skyhorse Publishing, 307 West 36th Street, 11th Floor, New York, NY 10018 or info@skyhorsepublishing.com.

Skyhorse® and Skyhorse Publishing® are registered trademarks of Skyhorse Publishing, Inc.®, a Delaware corporation.

Visit our website at www.skyhorsepublishing.com.

10 9 8 7 6 5 4 3 2 1

Library of Congress Cataloging-in-Publication Data is available on file.

Cover design by Jane Sheppard
Cover photo credit Christopher Kline

Print ISBN: 978-1-63220-288-8
Ebook ISBN: 978-1-63220-930-6

Printed in China

Contents

A special thanks to Dolores Kline, Dave Brigner, and Liz Coverdale for their editing and valuable feedback.

1
How to Use
This Book

Pepper and Salt Skipper

Chapter 1

How to Use This Book

Butterfly Gardening with Native Plants is intended to accomplish two goals. First, this book is to serve as an introduction to gardening, specifically with the purpose of attracting butterflies to your garden. In the mind of the butterfly, not all plants are created equal. In this book, I hope to encourage you to think like a butterfly.

Second, I want this book to serve as a butterfly field guide, specifically for the butterflies you are most likely to encounter in your garden in the eastern United States. For example, there are over 150 butterfly species native to the Ohio River valley. Not all of them will be making their way to your yard. However, for folks who have a little more experience with butterflies, there are some very good field guides that are available that will cover regional butterfly species much more comprehensively.

The beginning of the book discusses gardening, gardening style, and the importance of gardening. This is followed by the "field guide" portion of the book. In this section, all similar butterflies are grouped together. So, the butterfly section starts with the swallowtails, followed by the whites and sulphurs, blues and hairstreaks, brushfoots, and skippers.

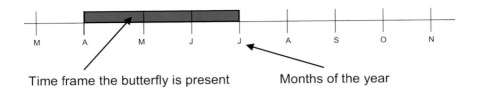

Time frame the butterfly is present   Months of the year

On each butterfly species page is a general description of the butterfly, its season, its host plant, and any specific advice about attracting the butterfly to your garden. At the top of the page is a bar that shows the season in which you would commonly find that butterfly. The letters across the bottom of the bar represent the months of the year.

The next section of the book discusses the best nectar plants for attracting butterflies, in rough order of bloom season. For each nectar plant, there is a general description of size and growth habit, sun requirements, and its specific attraction for butterflies. There is also

Variegated Fritillary

another calendar bar at the top showing the approximate bloom season of the plant.

In addition, certain plants have received "gold stars." These are my top ten, "must have" plants for any butterfly garden. My number one choice, Purple Milkweed, in my opinion, is the best butterfly attractant there is among our native flora.

The next section of the book contains a chart of butterfly host plants, or the plants that caterpillars of specific butterflies will eat. I like to think of caterpillars as nature's little pruners. The chart gives the name of the host plant, size, flower color, fall color, and the specific butterfly that feeds on the plant. Keep in mind, the purpose for having these plants in your garden is for them to be eaten. Do not invest $60 in a six-foot dogwood cultivar, when a $14.95, two-foot everyday dogwood will work. Do not worry, caterpillars will not eat your dogwood to the ground. They know better than to wipe out their food supply.

Finally, in the index, page numbers are listed not only for the page a particular species is discussed, but also pages in which a photo of a given plant or butterfly can be found. The page number in bold is the page number of the specific discussion of that species.

My hope is that through this book you will not only begin to notice the butterfly life around you, but that you will also take an active role in attracting that butterfly life to your home landscape. Many states and communities have butterfly clubs and Listservs that can help answer questions and provide encouragement. Good luck with your newfound butterfly interests!

2
Butterfly Gardening
Basics

Harvester

Chapter 2

Butterfly Gardening Basics

Why Gardening?

The practice of gardening dates back to Biblical times. One of the tasks assigned to Adam and Eve in the second chapter of Genesis was to "take care of it and keep it," in reference to the Garden of Eden.

Gardening is beneficial from a physical health perspective. When gardening, muscles are stretched and strengthened. Coordination and balance is challenged as one traverses narrow paths across the uneven ground. Joints are exercised as the gardener stoops and raises to work at different levels in the garden.

While these types of movements may seem minimal, their importance becomes more and more emphasized as our society and workplaces become more and more sedentary. We have escalators to move us vertically through space, and even horizontally through space in many airports. We use golf carts in the workplace to carry us and our equipment relatively short distances to which in the past we would've walked or ridden bicycles. Our hurried and busy lives have forced us into our cars to save time, when in the past we would've walked to nearby destinations.

Gardening not only provides physical benefits, it also provides emotional benefits. The idea of caring for and nurturing other forms of life takes us beyond our own selfish interests. As we care for our plants, we suddenly see ourselves as givers rather than takers. We suddenly realize we are needed, that these plants may die if not for our caring hands.

Our time in the garden allows us an escape from our normally busy and hectic lives. Much like a vacation to a distant place, we are able to lose ourselves in our gardens. While our garden may only be a few meters wide, we divide it mentally into sections; the butterfly section, the vegetable section, the ornamental grasses. Moving between sections is almost like catching a flight across the country, as each section has its own feel and personality.

Additionally, in our garden we are truly able to express ourselves. In our workplaces there is always someone who will feel the need to criticize an idea, to tell us, "No, you can't do the project that way, you must do it this way." Our gardens are our own. If we want to put the dill next to the milkweed, it is our decision to do so. If we want all the flowers in our garden to be yellow, we can do that, and nobody can take that decision away from us.

Our gardens are also a place of privacy. We can cry there, we can vent our anger there, we can contemplate our troubles or let our troubles fade into the distance. Forcefully removing a strongly entrenched weed gives us a feeling of power that we are frequently not permitted elsewhere in our lives.

Perhaps the greatest thing about gardening is that we can accomplish all these benefits for a rather small investment of money. A $1.29 package of seeds is far more affordable than a $100 per hour therapist. One therapy session can easily fund an entire backyard garden project, and the therapeutic effects of the garden can be enjoyed every day. No appointments required!

This is why gardening provides a physical and emotional release from the daily rigors. Gardening provides us with a sense of need, and it can carry us away to a different place, without the cost of a plane ticket.

Why Butterflies?

Why butterfly gardening, rather than vegetable gardening or herb gardening or flower gardening? I would like to give an analogy to answer this. In the elementary school setting, the study of science and social studies lends itself to cross-curricular approaches. The good scientist incorporates math, reading, and writing into his or her work. Field scientists even incorporate physical education. Good historians likewise must use other content areas to accomplish their tasks.

Butterfly gardening is the same. A good butterfly garden incorporates plants that one would normally find in an herb garden, such as dill, fennel, and parsley. A good butterfly garden incorporates plants that the gardener would use in a flower garden to achieve showy and spectacular displays, such as bee balm and milkweed. A good butterfly garden incorporates human food plants, such as sunflowers and wild cherries, as butterflies provide valuable pollination resources. With a good butterfly garden, you get to have your cake and eat it too!

Humans like to feel a sense of engagement with wildlife. How many people thrive on stories of the fish that got away, the bear sighting at Yellowstone Park, or a swim with beautiful tropical fish off the coast of a Caribbean island? If you have ever had the pleasure of a butterfly landing on your sweat soaked arm, you have most likely shared the story with your friends and family. Butterflies are all around us. All we need to do is notice.

Arizona Sister

I am reminded of a story a friend shared with me years ago. She and her foster children and a family friend had visited one of the sky islands of southern Arizona to escape the heat of Phoenix. As they walked back to their car along the mountain trail, an Arizona Sister butterfly landed on her son's arm, attracted by the mineral-rich salt from his sweat. The boy was quite pleased with his new hitchhiking friend. Not only did the hitchhiking Sister remain on the boy's arm the entire trip back to the car, but also as the boy got into the car and as the family drove part way down the road. The family finally stopped prior to leaving the habitat, opened the window, and forcibly chased the butterfly away.

Butterflies are safe. They cannot bite, claw, scratch, or infect you with an awful disease. All of us who have been scratched by the family cat, nipped by a friend's dog, or chased by a love-struck Canada Goose can appreciate the safety of butterflies.

I have researched monarch butterflies for several years. I have taught people age seven to seventy to tag monarchs and record data about them. One of my favorite things to do at the end of a children's tagging program is to release the monarch using a child's nose as the

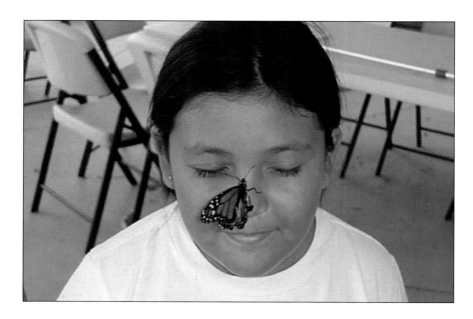

launch pad, much to the delight of both the children and adults in the group. If the research subject was a bear, cat, snake, scorpion, or other creature, I would not be able to provide for this sense of engagement.

Butterfly Life Cycle

Perhaps you have watched a butterfly bounce from plant to plant, landing on one leaf and then quickly moving on to the next leaf. Most likely this was a female looking for the correct plant on which to lay an egg. Butterflies will lay eggs only on very specific types of plants. These plants are known as host plants. Some butterfly species will lay a single egg at a time, while others may lay several eggs. Eggs are normally laid on the underside of leaves or on flower buds.

From the egg, a caterpillar will hatch. The caterpillar is only a few millimeters long when it hatches, and normally its first meal is its egg shell. Over the next few weeks, the caterpillar will eat its host plant, growing multitudes larger as it proceeds through five instars. A caterpillar sheds its skin as it moves into each instar. The fifth instar concludes when the caterpillar transforms into the chrysalis, or pupa stage, typically by hanging upside down from a branch, stem, or even a piece of rope, as I witnessed once in Portal, Arizona.

The chrysalis is a very vulnerable stage for the butterfly, as it has no mechanism to defend itself or escape from a predator. Consequently, the chrysalis relies on camouflage for protection, frequently appearing to be a dead or rolled up leaf, a small twig, or even a rock with sparkling crystals.

From this chrysalis, the adult butterfly will emerge, yet another very vulnerable stage in the insect's life. Initially, the butterfly's wings are useless and must be "pumped up" from fluid stored within its body. Once the wings are pumped up, they must then dry out. Therefore, a newly emerged butterfly is still a few hours away from being able to fly.

Butterflies are capable of over-wintering, living out the cold winter months, in any of the latter three stages. The time required to go through the four stages varies, depending on the species of butterfly. A monarch butterfly, for example, will require roughly 28 days to go from newly laid egg to adult. This timeframe can vary by a few days depending on food availability and weather. See the "Monarch" field guide entry on page 62 for images of these different stages.

Not everybody is a butterfly enthusiast. It would seem that the wild animal that many people relate to best is the bird. There were 61 million Americans who identified themselves as birdwatchers in the late 1980s. While it may seem sacrilegious to the butterfly enthusiasts, the truth is that butterfly and moth caterpillars are the best food for birds, even better than the one hundred pound bag of thistle seed you may have just purchased at the feed store.

Butterfly larva provide the fat and protein that growing nestlings and migrants need. Bird seed and fruits provide quickly burned carbohydrates. Bugs provide nutrients that seeds and fruits cannot provide. Your butterfly garden is actually the best bird garden you can provide.

Finally, butterflies fulfill a sense of nurturing. While I still lived in Arizona, I was slowly developing my own butterfly garden. One of the "weeds" in my garden was dogweed, *Dyssodia pentachaeta*. Dogweed is the larval host for the Dainty Sulphur, a dime-sized yellow butterfly. I would go out every Sunday morning and get down on hands and knees in the front yard examining the four-inch tall native dogweed, looking for caterpillars. I'm sure the neighbors questioned my sanity.

One of those Sundays, I found a Dainty Sulphur caterpillar. Now, every day upon getting home from work I would get down on hands and knees looking for *my* caterpillar. I watched it for several days until one day I could no longer find it. I wondered if it had become a protein shake for a local bird or if it had continued through its life cycle, now a chrysalis patiently waiting for the day that it would be visiting the flowers in my yard as an adult butterfly. Regardless, I was its Papa!

My Dainty Sulphur caterpillar!

Why Natives?

Throughout the United States, homeowners and developers have changed the face of the native landscape. In *Bringing Nature Home*, Douglas Tallamy estimates that over 62,500 square miles of the United

States have been converted from native habitat into lawn. This is slightly larger than the area of the state of Illinois.

The photo above is a Google Earth satellite image of a neighborhood in Canal Winchester, Ohio. The lawn in the upper left is nearly as large as a football field. Most homes in this neighborhood have a handful of trees at most, and virtually none have any nectar or larval hosts in their gardens.

While lawn may be pretty to look at for some, or fun to play on for others, through the eyes of a butterfly it may as well be a sand dune. Only four species of butterflies use bluegrass, the chief component of many lawns, as a caterpillar host species: Garita Skipperling, Juba Skipper, Least Skipper, and Long Dash. Of these four species, only the latter two are found in the Midwest. And of these two species, neither's caterpillars can survive being chopped in half by a lawnmower blade. No butterflies use grass as a nectar plant.

In addition, most of the plants, other than lawn, that we use to landscape our yards have European and Asian origins. Privet, lilac, and boxwood have all been introduced from elsewhere. It is estimated that 95 percent of the natural landscape has been turned unnatural by home landscaping and agricultural uses (Tallamy, 2007).

Unfortunately, our native insect fauna is generally not able to consume these Eurasian introductions. Plants contain various unpleasant chemicals, designed to protect them from chewing insects. However, as the local flora has developed these chemical defenses, the local insects have developed natural enzymes within their bodies to break down these chemicals. This is how insects help keep plant populations in check.

North American insects do not have the enzymes required to break down the nasty chemicals found within Eurasian plants. Consider Garlic Mustard, for example, an invasive member of the Brassicaceae (Mustard family) that was introduced into the United States as a culinary herb in the 1860s. Of the nearly seventy insect species that do have the enzymes to metabolize Garlic Mustard, all are found in the plant's home range of Europe, Asia, and Africa. Therefore, Garlic Mustard, thrives out of control in the eastern United States.

The use of exotic plants in our home landscapes, as well as the loss of native habitat, has reduced the biodiversity of the North American landscape significantly. Since we are all members of the same food web, this puts all organisms within the web at risk. Less native habitat

Garlic Mustard

means fewer insects, which means fewer birds, and so on.

The presence of exotic plants in one's home landscape was once considered a sign of wealth and prestige. Great expense and personal risk were required for explorers to bring beautiful exotic plants back to the botanical institutions of Europe and the East Coast of the United States. Greater expense and experimentation were then required to

Native, Viola sororia

make these plants available on a limited basis to the aristocrats of these regions. With advances in technology, twenty dollars is all that is required for anybody, aristocrat or not, to have Japanese Maple in their yard. This exotic-centric mentality, however, still persists today. Nurserymen carry exotic plants because that is what their customers request. Many nurserymen do not carry native plants because there is no demand for them. One of the goals for this book is to reintroduce native plants to the thinking of American homeowners.

Our native flora is directly linked to our native fauna. Native oaks host seventeen species of butterfly caterpillars across the United States. Native violets host twenty-two species of butterfly caterpillars. If we add moth caterpillars to the tally, native oaks host a whopping 534 species of Lepidoptera. Wild black cherry hosts another 456 species of Lepidoptera. It becomes obvious that by replacing exotic species like Garlic Mustard with native species like violets, which also serve as a culinary herb, one can increase the wildlife value of their home landscape exponentially! It is a case of having your cake and literally eating it too!

There is also a mentality that exotic plants are prettier than our local natives. However, I challenge anyone to find an exotic that is brighter and bolder than most of our native milkweeds, Joe Pyes, or ironweeds. Many of our native grasses are just as lovely as the ornamental grasses we import from across the ocean.

Another problem with exotic species, as mentioned earlier, is that they tend to escape the controlled garden environment and become invasive in the native landscape. Honeysuckle poppers have been invented to remove invasive Asian honeysuckles from the American landscape. In the mountains around Tucson, Arizona, local residents now have weed-whacking parties on weekends, going into the mountains north and east of town to pull up invasive grasses, which create significant fire hazards around foothill housing developments.

At what point will we need to arrive before we realize that native plants and animals are necessary for a healthy ecosystem? The time is now to practice good land stewardship, and the place is our own backyards!

3
Garden Design
Basics

American Copper

Chapter 3

Garden Design Basics

Arrangement

While the way in which you arrange your butterfly garden will not affect the butterflies' enjoyment and utilization of the space, it will most certainly affect your enjoyment of the space. As you arrange your butterfly garden, keep in mind that larger plants should go toward the back of the space. By doing this, you will be able to view all of the plants in the space. For an island style garden, the larger plants should be placed in the middle to allow for viewing from any direction.

Also keep in mind that, unlike the butterflies, you must enter the space on foot. Paths should be planned for, so that you can access the entire space without stepping on plants and potentially caterpillars.

Nectar plants and larval food plants do not need to be directly next to each other. Butterflies have an uncanny way of finding their preferred larval food plants. However, placing a large house or woodlot in between the two could be problematic. Placing nectar and larval food plants within a relatively short flight from each other will encourage a longer visit to your butterfly garden.

Textures

While your choice of plants will be dictated more by the butterfly species you are hoping to attract, plant textures must be a consideration regarding placement. For a feeling of continuity, like textures at the same vertical level should be placed together. For example, a coarse-leaved plant, such as canna lily, will look awkward next to a wispy native grass of the same height. Instead, place the canna lily on one side of the garden while using the native grass on the opposite side. For an island bed, consider using a large shrub or small tree in the middle to create a buffer between coarse-leaved and fine-leaved plants.

Texture is not as much of a concern when plants are of varying heights. For example, ferns towering over a hosta plant can look quite attractive, despite the fact that the fern has a wispy texture while the hosta has a much coarser texture. While the plants may be next to each other, their textures do not compete because they are at differing vertical levels.

Color

Butterflies are attracted to a wide variety of colors. Remember, to a butterfly, the color of the flower is not nearly as important as the tubular shape of the flower. In addition, butterflies can see wavelengths beyond the human eye's visible spectrum. What you think is a white flower may look totally different to a butterfly. Typically, color is more important to the butterfly gardener, so use specific colors that you find appealing. Remember, the butterfly garden is not only a place of nurturing, it is also a place of healing and expression for you.

With this said, different colors are known to evoke different emotions. Whites, pinks, purples, and blues tend to have a calming and peaceful effect. Yellows, reds, and oranges tend to evoke excitement and happiness. If your normal day tends toward the hectic and chaotic side of the continuum, you may wish to guide your garden to the cooler, more peaceful and calming colors. If your normal day tends toward the monotonous and boring, you may emphasize the brighter, more exciting colors.

Balance

Your butterfly garden will be more emotionally comfortable for you if it is properly balanced. Several tall perennials or shrubs on one side of the garden with only ground covers on the other side will appear unbalanced and awkward. But, by simply adding a small tree to the ground cover side, one can achieve a greater sense of balance. Balance does not mean that one side looks exactly like the other.

Hardscaping

Hardscaping refers to the nonvegetative aspects of your garden, including rocks, pathways, and borders. As you design your butterfly garden, keep in mind that you will need a series of paths that will allow access to the different areas of the garden. What will be the material you use for these paths? Mulch? Flagstone? Patio stones? Pea gravel?

A mulch path is perhaps the easiest method. Simply put down a layer of mulch a few inches thick. The mulch will need to be added to over time as the material begins to compress and decompose. A thick layer of mulch will also deter weeds, although some weeding may still be required. However, mulch may become soggy and muddy during periods of great rainfall.

Flagstone, patio stones, and pea gravel are more likely to keep your feet dry but require more preparation work. Once you have decided where the paths will go, mark the paths in the garden area using flags or stakes. Then remove about two inches of soil from the length of the path. In the bottom of this "trench," place roughly an inch of sand. The sand will provide a firm base upon which to place the stepping stones, whether they be flagstone, patio stones, or another substrate entirely.

Different materials will be available in different areas. In some areas, crushed granite or crushed limestone may be available as the path tread. Use a compactor or roller to compress the substrate to make it solid under foot. Another benefit to using granite or limestone is that male butterflies will use this material for puddling. Puddling is a behavior that males exhibit when they gather in large numbers to sip mineral-rich water through their proboscis. This mineral-rich water helps in the formation of spermatophores.

If using flagstone or patio stones, place the stones on the sand bed at a distance apart from each other that allows for comfortable stepping

Sample Design I—General Butterfly Garden

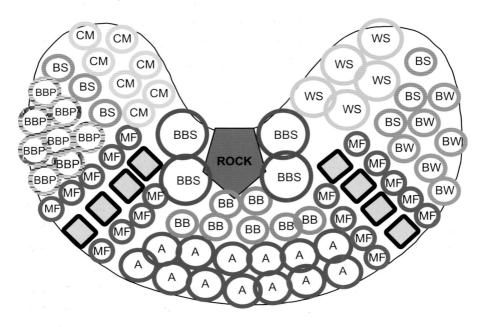

Sample Design I—General Butterfly Garden

Plants Codes:
A - Aster
BB - Bee Balm (Monarda)
BBP - Bluebells/Parsley
BBS - Big Bluestem
BS - Blazing Star

BW - Butterfly Weed
CM - Common Milkweed
MF - Mistflower
WS - Wingstem

from stone to stone. Then use additional sand or pea gravel to fill the space between the stones. Avoid using wood as your path tread. Not only will it rot over time, as the wood gets wet it will eventually be covered with algae, which will make it slippery and hazardous.

Boulders are often used in the butterfly garden as well, providing a basking spot for both human and lepidopteran users of the space.

The General Butterfly Garden is designed to appeal to both the nectar needs and host plant needs of Midwestern butterflies. All of the plants in this design, with the exception of Big Bluestem and parsley, will meet butterfly nectar needs throughout the season. Bluebells will provide early season nectar, while the large planting of aster in the middle will provide late season nectar. The other nectar sources will provide nectar throughout the summer.

As the Bluebells fade in late spring, plant parsley to serve as a host plant for Black Swallowtails. Big Bluestem is a tall prairie grass found throughout the Midwest and is used by many skippers as a host plant. In addition, the Common Milkweed and Butterfly Weed serve as monarch butterfly hosts. Wingstem is a host for the Silvery Checkerspot, while aster is a host for the Pearl Crescent.

If you study the arrangement of this garden, the Big Bluestem provides a central focal point. Big Bluestem will grow to six to seven feet in height. The large rock flanked by the bluestem not only adds to the focal point but also provides a perching site for butterflies.

The tallest remaining plants, Common Milkweed and Wingstem, are to the back and sides of the space. This way, they do not interfere with viewing any of the other plant material and make a colorful backdrop for the garden as a whole.

The Bee Balm and Blazing Stars provide a transition between taller plants to the back and shorter plants to the front. This will give your garden the appearance of a stair-step effect.

In this design, patio stones are used for the access paths into the garden. A mulch or gravel path could just as easily play the role. Mistflower, one of the shorter plants in the garden, makes a nice edge for the walking path and will provide late summer color.

In this garden, plants have been packed tightly together, which provides a mass of color rather than individual splotches of color. To save money, and provide more space for moving within the garden, certainly try planting more sparsely. However, planting too far apart will provide a greater opportunity for weeds and take away from the color mass.

Sample Design II—Caterpillar Garden

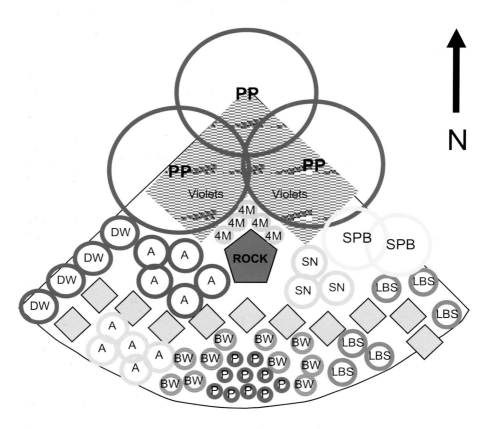

Sample Design II—Caterpillar Garden

Plants Codes:
A - Aster
DW - Dogwood
P - Parsley
SN - Senna
4M - Four-leaved Milkweed

BW - Butterfly Weed
LBS - Little Bluestem
PP - Pawpaw
SPB - Spicebush

 The Caterpillar Garden is designed specifically to meet the needs of the larval stage of the butterfly. While the focus may be on caterpillars, there is still plenty of nectar as well, as aster, Butterfly Weed, and Four-leaved Milkweed are all excellent nectar sources. Pawpaw is a small- to medium-sized tree that creates quite a bit of shade. It is the caterpillar host plant of the Zebra Swallowtail. Another feature of Pawpaw is that the fruit, also known as the Hoosier Banana, is edible, and quite tasty.

In the shade created by the Pawpaw, violets are planted. Violets are a woodland wildflower with many different species. Flower color also varies widely, including white, yellow, and various shades of purple. Violets are the caterpillar host plant for several fritillary butterflies. Also in the shade of the Pawpaw is Four-leaved Milkweed, one of the few milkweeds that is tolerant of shady conditions. Of course, milkweed is the host of the monarch butterfly.

In the design, dogwood on the left side balances with Spicebush on the right. Dogwood is a host for Spring and Summer Azures while Spicebush is the host for the Spicebush Swallowtail.

For variety, the design encourages the use of both white and purple asters. Heath Aster is among the more common of the white species, while New England Aster is perhaps the most recognized of the purple.

Butterfly Weed, a species of milkweed, surrounds a planting of parsley. While not native, parsley, a member of the carrot family of plants, is included to attract Black Swallowtails. Many of our wild carrots are not conducive to garden use because of their extreme size, invasive tendencies, and toxicity.

The front right corner includes a large planting of Little Bluestem, a native prairie grass. Native grasses are used by various skippers and satyrs as a host plant.

Senna provides a backdrop for the grasses. Senna provides food for the caterpillars of several species of sulphur butterflies, including Little Yellow, Sleepy Orange, and Cloudless Sulphur.

Sample Design III—Monarch Garden

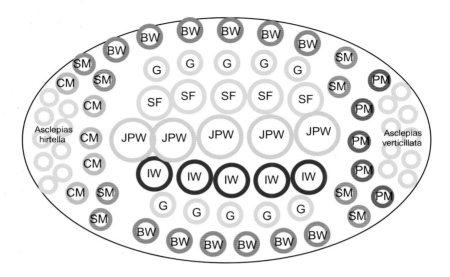

Sample Design III—Monarch Garden

Plants Codes:
BW - Butterfly Weed
G - Goldenrod
JPW - Joe Pye Weed
SF - Sunflower

CM - Common Milkweed
IW - Ironweed
PM - Purple Milkweed
SM - Swamp Milkweed

The Monarch Garden is designed specifically to meet the needs of the monarch butterfly. The monarch is famous for its long migration every fall. Monarchs from the Midwest migrate to the Transvolcanic Mountain Range northwest of Mexico City. While there, monarchs spend the winter clustering within the Oyumel Fir trees.

In the Monarch Garden, late season nectar plants have been specifically chosen. Joe Pye Weed, Ironweed, sunflower, and goldenrod all bloom in late summer to early autumn. These plants will help provide valuable food resources for migrating monarchs.

This garden is packed with a large variety of milkweeds to be utilized as caterpillar food sources. At each end of the garden are lower growing milkweeds, Asclepias hirtella (Prairie Milkweed) and Asclepias verticillata (Whorled Milkweed). Each of these species grow 18 to 24 inches tall with whitish flowers. On the left side of the garden, Common Milkweed, perhaps the most commonly used host plant for wild monarchs, provides a backdrop. On the right side of the garden, Purple Milkweed provides a backdrop. Butterfly Weed provides both a strong caterpillar and nectar food source along the front and back of the space. Swamp Milkweed is scattered in the corners of the garden to provide further variety.

It is important to note that this garden is designed for viewing from all sides and, to an extent, is four different spaces combined into one. When standing in front of either end, the view is contained with shorter plants in front and taller in the back; likewise, when standing in the front or back facing the Butterfly Weed. The Joe Pye Weed provides the "back" of the space.

There are no specific paths designed to take the gardener throughout this space. However, since the space readily divides itself into fourths, access from any direction should be easy. Once again, plant density can be decreased to an extent to allow for greater access.

Not only does the Monarch Garden provide a cornucopia of milkweed choices for monarch caterpillars, but it also provides a wealth of nectar for all butterflies from early summer through the monarch migration season in early autumn.

4
Common Butterflies in the Garden

Pearl Crescent

Chapter 4

Common Butterflies in the Garden

Zebra Swallowtail
Eurytides marcellus

| M | A | M | J | J | A | S | O | N |

Description
This swallowtail is very pale, cream-color to nearly white with dark stripes. Summer Zebras (second brood) have longer tails than spring Zebras.

Season
One of the first butterflies to emerge in the spring. Zebras are common until early to mid-summer.

Habitat
Zebra Swallowtails frequent open areas like lawns and fields as well as wooded edges and wooded roads.

Host Plant
Pawpaw (*Asimina triloba*). A small tree that grows to 15 feet

in sun or shade. The range of this tropical tree species extends north into southern Ohio and Indiana.

Attracting to Your Garden

Planting Pawpaw in your yard is the best way to attract this beautiful early season butterfly. Milkweed is a strong nectar attractant for this species.

Pawpaw fruit (Host)

Eastern Tiger Swallowtail
Papilio glaucus

| M | A | M | J | J | A | S | O | N |

Description

This swallowtail has a base color of pale to bright yellow with dark stripes and orange and blue eye spots. Size varies from four to five inches across. Females of the species also have a dark form, which is more common to the south.

dark form female

Season

One of the first butterflies to emerge in the spring. Tigers are common spring through fall.

yellow form male

Habitat

Tiger Swallowtails frequent open areas like lawns and fields as well as wooded edges and wooded roads. Tigers are also the puddling champions of Midwestern butterflies, sometimes attracting several dozen to a single mudhole.

Host Plant

Various hardwood trees, including Cottonwood (*Populus deltoides*), Tulip Tree (*Liriodendron tulipifera),* and cherry (*Prunus serotina*).

Attracting to Your Garden

If host trees are available nearby, all that is needed are nectar plants to attract adults. A nice mudhole or wet sandy spot will also encourage Tigers to visit.

Tulip Tree blossom (host)

Spicebush Swallowtail
Papilio troilus

M   A   M   J   J   A   S   O   N

Description

This dark swallowtail lacks yellow on the upper surface but has plenty of iridescent blue and pale blue spots. On the underside of the hindwing, look for two rows of orange spots to distinguish this species from Pipevine Swallowtail.

Season

Look for this butterfly in late spring and throughout summer.

Spicebush (host)

Habitat

Spicebush Swallowtail prefers wooded habitats and small openings in woods.

Host Plant

Spicebush (*Lindera benzoin*). This is a common woodland shrub except in the extreme north of the region.

Attracting to Your Garden

Planting Spicebush in your yard is the best way to attract this beautiful butterfly. Home landscapes that are open with few trees will struggle attracting this species.

Black Swallowtail
Papilio polyxenes

| M | A | M | J | J | A | S | O | N |

Description
Males have a distinct row of yellow dots across the top of both the fore- and hindwings. Females lack yellow and strongly resemble the Spicebush Swallowtail. Look for an orange spot at base of upper hindwing, and pale spots on lower forewing.

Season
One of the first butterflies to emerge in the spring, flying through late summer.

Black Swallowtail caterpillar

Habitat
Black Swallowtails frequent open areas like lawns, fields, and gardens.

Host Plant
Black Swallowtails will lay eggs on both wild and garden members of the carrot family, including dill, fennel, parsley, and carrot. Wild members of this family tend to be quite large, dense colonizers, and toxic. Wild members include Poison Hemlock, Water Hemlock, and Cow Parsnip. Using garden herbs is strongly suggested over wild plants or Queen Anne's Lace, an invasive introduction.

Attracting to Your Garden
An open home landscape with garden plants that include members of the carrot family will surely attract this beautiful butterfly.

Cabbage White
Pieris rapae

M	A	M	J	J	A	S	O	N

Description

This small white butterfly is an introduction from Europe. Look for dark forewing tips, black dots on upper forewing, and creamy white underwings lacking any dark shadow on the veins. This species is quite common, but can be confused in our area with

Native Mustards, Spring Cress (host)

the Checkered White (look for dark veining on underside of hindwing) and the West Virginia White (no dark spots on upper wing surfaces).

Season

One of the first butterflies to emerge in the spring and flies through late summer and fall.

Habitat

Look for Cabbage Whites in open fields, lawns, and garden areas.

Host Plant

This species will lay eggs on various members of the mustard family, including garden vegetables cabbage and broccoli. In more wild environs, they will use a variety of native mustards, including *Cardamine* and *Arabis*.

Attracting to Your Garden

These butterflies are so common that no extra effort is required to attract them; they'll find you!

Orange Sulphur
Colias eurytheme

M   A   M   J   J   A   S   O   N

Description

Orange Sulphur is very similar to Clouded Sulphur. This species will flash orange from its upper forewing when in flight. In western portions of the Midwest, this species could be confused with Sleepy Orange. Look for brown/red splotching on the underneath surface of the Sleepy hindwing.

Season

This species appears in mid-spring and continues flying throughout summer and into fall.

Habitat

Look for Orange Sulphur in open fields, lawns, and gardens.

Host Plant

Alfalfa and clover. Clover is a common constituent of most lawns and fields; however, the frequent mowing of lawns makes clover unsuitable for caterpillar survival.

Attracting to Your Garden

No special effort is required to attract this butterfly to your butterfly garden. With the abundance of alfalfa and clover comes an abundance of Orange Sulphurs. Even a minute nectar supply will attract this species.

Clouded Sulphur
Colias philodice

| M | A | M | J | J | A | S | O | N |

Description
Clouded Sulphur is frustratingly similar to Orange Sulphur. Clouded Sulphur will lack the flash of orange on the upper wing surface. While sitting at rest, it is nearly impossible to distinguish Orange from Clouded Sulphur.

Season
This species appears in mid-spring and continues flying throughout summer and into fall.

Habitat
Look for Clouded Sulphur in open fields, lawns, and gardens.

Host Plant
Alfalfa and clover.

Attracting to Your Garden
No special effort is required to attract this butterfly to your butterfly garden. With the abundance of alfalfa and clover comes an abundance of Clouded Sulphurs.

Alfalfa (host)

Cloudless Sulphur
Phoebis sennae

| M | A | M | J | J | A | S | O | N |

Description
This lemon yellow butterfly is larger than other sulphurs. Typically there are no obvious dark markings on the upper surface of the wings and only a few blemishes on the underneath surface of the wings.

Season
Cloudless Sulphurs migrate north into the Ohio River

Valley from farther south, typically arriving in the middle of summer.

Habitat
Look for this species in garden and wildflower rich areas in the southern and western portions of the range.

Host Plant
Senna (*Senna hederacea*). This perennial prefers sunny locations and will grow to five feet high.

Northern Wild Senna (host)

Attracting to Your Garden

Planting the larval host plant Senna is your best bet to attract this species in mid- and late-summer. A robust supply of summer-blooming nectar plants is also critical.

Coral Hairstreak
Satyrium titus

M A M J J A S O N

Description

This small gray hairstreak is the size of a nickel in profile. Look for a row of orange dots on the lower surface of the hindwing to distinguish this species from other hairstreaks. The slender tails on the hindwings of most hairstreaks are absent in the Coral Hairstreak.

Season

Look for this hairstreak during the summer.

Wild Black Cherry blossom (host)

Habitat

Coral Hairstreaks frequent brushy areas as well as garden areas.

Host Plant

Wild Cherry (*Prunus serotina*). This tree species is common throughout the Ohio River Valley. It prefers sun to partial shade and grows to 70 feet high.

Attracting to Your Garden

The key to attracting this species is planting Butterfly Weed, *Asclepias tuberosa*, in your garden. You also want Wild Cherry in your yard or neighborhood.

Gray Hairstreak
Strymon melinus

M A M J J A S O N

Description

This hairstreak is slightly larger than a dime in profile. Look for two orange spots on the underneath surface of the hindwing. The submarginal lines on both wings are dark with orange to the inside and white to the outside. As with many hairstreaks, the slender tails frequently break off over time.

Season

Look for Gray Hairstreaks from June through mid- to late-summer.

Habitat

Gray Hairstreaks frequent brushy areas as well as garden areas.

Host Plant

Gray Hairstreaks eat the flower portions of many species of plants, including mallows and legumes, such as clover.

Attracting to Your Garden

This species seems to prefer Wingstem (*Verbesinia alternifolia*) as a nectar plant. Nearby meadows with clovers and native legumes will also increase your chances of attracting this tiny beauty.

Eastern Tailed Blue
Cupido comyntas

M   A   M   J   J   A   S   O   N

Description

The Eastern Tailed Blue is the size of a dime in profile and is one of the few blues with tails. The upper surface of the wings is blue in males, gray in females. Look for two orange spots near the hindwing tails. Ants attend the caterpillars of various blues, collecting "honeydew" from them and in return protecting the caterpillar from predation.

Season

Look for Eastern Tailed Blues throughout the entire butterfly season.

Habitat

Look for this species in lawns, gardens, and parks, especially near clover.

Host Plant

Legume family members, including clover, crownvetch, and so forth.

Attracting to Your Garden

Crownvetch (host)

While lawn grasses will not attract this species, the weeds that grow in your yard, mainly clover, will attract Eastern Tailed Blues. Leave the weed and feed in the garage and let the clover come up in the lawn.

Spring/Summer Azure
Celastrina ladon/C. neglecta

| M | A | M | J | J | A | S | O | N |

Description

Spring and Summer Azures are very difficult to tell apart. Both are small gray butterflies with blue on the upper wing surface. Spring Azure flies in spring and has bold, dark markings on the underside of the wings. Summer Azure flies in summer and has more subtle dark markings.

Spring Azure

Season

Spring Azure is present in spring, Summer Azure in summer. One or the other is viewable throughout the entire butterfly season.

Habitat

These small butterflies can be found everywhere, including woodlots, gardens, lawns, and fields.

Host Plant

Azure larva feed on a wide variety of flowers, primarily dogwood, but will also utilize Viburnum and cherry.

Summer Azure

Attracting to Your Garden

The Azures will find their own way to your garden, but to provide better viewing of them, try creating a puddling area for them, as the males of this species are notorious for puddling behaviors. Also maintain a variety of native shrubs and small trees with varying blooming seasons to provide plenty of food for developing caterpillars.

Great Spangled Fritillary
Speyeria cybele

| | | | | | | | | |
|M|A|M|J|J|A|S|O|N|

Description

This large fritillary can be easily confused with the Aphrodite Fritillary. On the Great Spangled, look for a cream-colored band that connects the two outer rows of silver dots on the underside of the hind-wing (indicated below with red arrow). In Aphrodite, this band does not touch both rows of dots.

Season

Great Spangled is very common but in a very limited window of time. Look for this species to be most prolific when milkweed is blooming in summer.

Habitat

Fields, gardens, and woodlot edges.

Host Plant

Violets (*Viola sp.*). There are many species of violet, ranging in flower color from purple to yellow to white.

Violet

Attracting to Your Garden

Great Spangled Fritillaries love to nectar on milkweed. In fact, several will share the same milkweed umbel. If you plant milkweed, they will come!

Aphrodite Fritillary
Speyeria aphrodite

M | A | M | J | J | A | S | O | N

Description
Easily confused with the Great Spangled Fritillary, the Aphrodite is smaller, and the cream-colored band on the underside of the hindwing is narrower, not connecting the two rows of silver dots.

Season
Look for Aphrodite in early to mid-summer.

Habitat
Woodlot edges, fields, and gardens.

Host Plant
Violets (*Viola sp.*). Note that violets come in a variety of different species and colors. Most flower in spring, but the leaves remain well into summer, providing a valuable summer food source for growing caterpillars.

Violet (host)

Attracting to Your Garden
In the natural world of the Midwest, milkweed is the primary summer nectar source. Plant milkweed to improve your chances of attracting this beautiful orange butterfly.

Meadow Fritillary
Boloria bellona

| M | A | M | J | J | A | S | O | N |

Description

The smallest of the three fritillaries common in the Midwest, the Meadow Fritillary has no silver dots on the underside of the hindwing. The upper wing surface looks very similar to the Aphrodite and Great Spangled.

Season

The Meadow Fritillary, while being the least common of the three fritillaries mentioned here, has the largest window of observation. Meadow Frits may be encountered from late spring through to late summer.

Habitat

Fields and woodlot edges.

Violet (host)

Host Plant

Violets (*Viola sp.*). Note that violets come in a variety of different species and colors, although most flower in spring.

Attracting to Your Garden

This species is not as attracted to summer milkweed as the other fritillaries. A substantial planting of violets and a more "wild" or brushy section of your garden will improve your chances.

Pearl Crescent
Phyciodes tharos

M A M J J A S O N

Description

No other small, eastern, orange butterfly has the bold dark lines on the orange background like the Pearl Crescent. The Pearl Crescent is possibly the most common butterfly in the Midwest.

Season

Pearl Crescent flies throughout the butterfly season.

Habitat

Everywhere! While this butterfly seems to prefer more open habitats like fields, gardens, and lawns, it can also be found along woodlot edges.

Host Plant

Aster. There are many species of aster, ranging in flower color from purple, to pale-purple, to white. A color to match every gardener's color scheme!

Attracting to Your Garden

The Pearl Crescent is so common, no extra effort is required to attract them. However, a section of your garden dedicated to aster will keep your Crescents in residence. A variety of nectar sources will keep the species coming back to your garden all season long.

Aster (Host)

Eastern Comma
Polygonia comma

| M | A | M | J | J | A | S | O | N |

Description

The Eastern Comma belongs to the group of brushfoots known as Anglewings, due to the sharply angled wing edges. The silvery comma on the back of the hindwing gives this species away. This species actually overwinters as an adult, spending the cold winter in brush piles or behind loose pieces of tree bark.

Season

Spring through fall. One of the first butterflies to emerge in spring and one of the last to hibernate in fall.

Habitat

Woodlots and streamsides.

Host Plant

Elm (*Ulmus Americana*) and nettle (*Urtica sp.*) Be careful when examining *Urtica* for caterpillars as most species have sharp bristles that will inflict a painful sting. For this reason, using *Urtica* in your garden is discouraged.

Attracting to Your Garden

The Eastern Comma is far more likely to fly over your butterfly garden than to land in it. Not known to visit flowers, try leaving rotting fruit in the garden to attract this species. Gardens near woods will fare better. This species hibernates during the winter and may fly on a warm winter day.

Question Mark
Polygonia interrogationis

M   A   M   J   J   A   S   O   N

Description

This anglewing differs from the Eastern Comma by having longer tails on the hindwings, which can be broken off, and a silvery "question mark" on the underside of the hind wing. On the upper wing surface, look for a "dash" above the three dots.

Season

Another of the winter hibernating butterflies, Question Marks are among the first butterflies to appear in spring and will fly through to fall.

Habitat

The Question Mark is much more wide ranging than the Comma, visiting woodlots, streamsides, parks, and gardens.

Host Plant

A varied diet, including elm (*Ulmus americana*), nettle (*Urtica sp.*), hops (*Humulus sp.*), and Hackberry (*Celtis reticulata*).

Attracting to Your Garden

Not known for flower nectaring, try rotting fruit in the garden. Availability of puddling areas will also attract this species.

Humulus (Host)

Common Buckeye
Junonia coenia

M   A   M   J   J   A   S   O   N

Description

In the Midwest, there is no other butterfly that can be confused with the Common Buckeye and its large eyespots on the upper wing surface. The Buckeye, along with the Comma, is one of the last butterflies to disappear in autumn.

Season

Look for Buckeyes from mid-summer through autumn.

Habitat

Buckeyes are a common visitor to fields, meadows, and even urban gardens.

Host Plant

Buckeyes utilize a variety of host plants, including Speedwells (*Veronica*), Monkeyflower (*Mimulus*), and *Plantago*. Many of these host plants qualify more as lawn weeds than wildflowers; however, *Mimulus ringens* is quite attractive.

Attracting to Your Garden

A variety of nectar plants, especially plants in the sunflower and mint families, will virtually guarantee a visit from these showy flyers.

Mimulus ringens (host)

Red Admiral
Vanessa atalanta

M   A   M   J   J   A   S   O   N

Description
The Red Admiral is most easily recognized by the orange/red horseshoe design on the upper surface of the wings.

Season
Look for this butterfly late spring through fall.

Habitat
Red Admirals will frequent woodland clearings and edges, parks, and gardens. Do not look for this species in heavy woodlots. Red Admirals are especially common in streamside habitats.

Host Plant
Nettle (*Urtica sp.*), Pellitory (*Parietaria sp.*), and False Nettle (*Boehmeria cylindrica*). Each of these species are common in wooded, streamside habitats.

Attracting to Your Garden
The Red Admiral is known for traveling great distances, so the key to bringing this butterfly to your garden is having plenty of nectar.

False Nettle (Host)

Painted Lady
Vanessa cardui

| M | A | M | J | J | A | S | O | N |

Description

The Painted Lady is easily confused with the American Lady. On the upper hindwing surface, the Painted Lady has four similarly sized blue eye spots. On the lower hindwing surface, once again look for four similarly sized eyespots (compare to the American Lady next page).

Season

Look for this butterfly late spring through fall.

Habitat

Painted Ladies will frequent woodland clearings and edges, parks, and gardens. Do not look for this species in heavy woodlots.

Host Plant

Thistle (*Cirsium sp.*) and mallows.

Attracting to Your Garden

The Painted Lady is also known for traveling great distances, so do not skimp on the nectar.

Cirsium discolor (host)

American Lady
Vanessa virginiensis

M	A	M	J	J	A	S	O	N	

Description

The American Lady is easily confused with the Painted Lady. On the upper hindwing surface, the American Lady has four blue eye spots, the end spots noticeably larger than the others. On the lower hindwing surface, look for two large eyespots at the edge of a cobwebby mass of lines.

Season

Look for this butterfly late spring through fall.

Habitat

American Ladies will frequent woodland clearings and edges, parks, and gardens. Do not look for this species in heavy woodlots.

Pussytoes (Host)

Host Plant

Everlastings (*Gnaphalium sp.*) and Pussytoes (*Antennaria sp.*).

Attracting to Your Garden

The American Lady will be attracted by large masses of color, especially sunflower-like flowers, such as Wingstem and goldenrod.

Hackberry Emperor
Asterocampa celtis

| M | A | M | J | J | A | S | O | N |

Description
The Hackberry Emperor is chocolate brown on the upper surface with blue eye spots along the border of each wing.

Season
Look for this butterfly late spring through fall.

Habitat
This butterfly typically perches in trees; therefore, it is more common in wood-lots and wooded edges. It will also frequent parks and gardens with plenty of trees.

Host Plant
Hackberry (*Celtis occidentalis*). Hackberry can become quite a large tree, to 60 feet high.

Hackberry (host) in fall foliage

Attracting to Your Garden
Hackberry trees near your home or in your neighborhood are the best insurance to attract this lovely Emperor. Look for this butterfly perching in trees near your garden. Placing rotting fruit in your garden will also attract Emperors. The Hackberry Emperor is also quite bold in its relationship with people, dive-bombing humans that enter its territory or stopping to steal a salty drink from a sweaty t-shirt (left)!

Red-spotted Purple
Limenitis arthemis

M A M J J A S O N

Description

The Red-spotted Purple has dark upper forewings with iridescent blue on the upper hindwing. Also look for faint red spots near the tip of the upper forewing. Notice that this butterfly has no hindwing tails, as the Red-spotted Purple looks very similar to some of our dark swallowtails.

Season

Look for this butterfly late spring through fall.

Habitat

The Red-spotted Purple prefers open areas and openings in woodlots.

Host Plant

Willow (*Salix sp.*) and Cottonwood (*Populus deltoids*). There are many different species of willow available at garden centers in a wide variety of growth habits and sizes. Plan on having to give them water during dry periods, however. Cottonwood becomes a huge tree, the size of which most home landscapes cannot accomodate. Cottonwood roots also tend to invade underground water pipes.

Attracting to Your Garden

This butterfly prefers perching on gravel and sandy surfaces. Creating puddling habitats will improve the chances of attracting this beautiful butterfly.

Viceroy
Limenitis archippus

| M | A | M | J | J | A | S | O | N |

Description
The Viceroy closely resembles the monarch. Look for a black arch on the orange/brown background of the upper hindwing.

Season
Look for this species late spring through early autumn.

Habitat
Streamside habitats and wooded edges.

Host Plant
Willow (*Salix sp.*). There are many different species of willow available at garden centers in a wide variety of growth habits and sizes. Plan on having to give them water during dry periods, however.

Attracting to Your Garden
Home landscapes near wooded streams will have the best chance of attracting these monarch impersonators. Also try planting willow in your butterfly garden. Viceroys are not known for visiting nectar.

Willow blossom (Host)

Monarch
Danaus plexippus

M   A   M   J   J   A   S   O   N

Description

The monarch is easily recognized as our primary big orange butterfly. Be sure to look for the absence of a black arch on the hindwings to distinguish this species from the Viceroy. The monarch is also famous for its long-distance migrations.

Season

The farther north, the later monarchs appear. In the spring, plan on monarchs appearing mid-May along the Ohio River. By early October, most monarchs have begun their migration south.

Habitat

Monarchs prefer open fields and gardens where milkweed is present. Habitat also distinguishes this species from the Viceroy, as Viceroys prefer streamsides and wooded edges.

Chrysalis

Host Plant

Milkweed, primarily Common Milkweed (*Asclepias syriaca*), but other milkweeds are also used.

Attracting to Your Garden

Planting milkweed will nearly guarantee this visitor to the garden!

Caterpillar

Little Wood Satyr
Megisto cymela

| M | A | M | J | J | A | S | O | N |

Description
This small brown butterfly is easily recognized by the pair of eye-spots on the upper surface of each wing. While this species has a brief window during the year for observation, typically they are present in great numbers.

Season
Look for Little Wood Satyr from early to mid-summer.

Habitat
Little Wood Satyrs prefer grassy areas with scattered trees. They can also be found along wooded edges.

Host Plant
A variety of native grasses, including the Purpletop shown below.

Attracting to Your Garden
A large planting of native grasses will be your best bet to attract this summertime gem.

Purpletop grass (Host)

Common Wood Nymph
Cercyonis pegale

| M | A | M | J | J | A | S | O | N |

Description
The yellow patch on the forewing will catch your eye and confirm your identification of this woodland butterfly. Look for this butterfly in trees, as they rarely visit flowers.

Season
Common Wood Nymphs are strictly a summer species.

Habitat
Look for the Common Wood Nymph along woodlot edges and grassy woodlands.

Host Plant
A variety of native grasses.

Attracting to Your Garden

A large planting of grasses, such as this hilltop in southeast Ohio, with nearby trees will be your best bet to attract this beauty. Be sure, however, to use grasses native to your area. Local butterflies frequently do not lay eggs on exotic grasses, plus many exotic grasses carry a high potential for becoming invasive.

Duskywings
Erynnis sp.

M   A   M   J   J   A   S   O   N

Description

There are several species of duskywings in our area, and they are all small, brown, and rarely hold still long enough to get a good look at them. To distinguish between duskywings, a good look at the glassy spots in the forewing is required. Pictured to the left is Dreamy Duskywing. A comprehensive butterfly guide is required to distinguish between duskywing species.

Dreamy Duskywing

Mournful Duskywing

Season

Early spring through late summer.

Habitat

Open areas, including lawns, gravel roads, parks, and gardens.

Host Plants

There are nine different duskywing species you could potentially encounter in the range covered by this book. Those nine have a variety of host plants but most of the nine use oaks (*Quercus sp.*), and legume species such as Crownvetch (*Coronilla varia*), as hosts. Keep in mind that Crownvetch is actually a naturalized exotic species not native to our area.

Attracting to Your Garden

These small skippers will find your garden on their own. Do not pull up those dandelions in your grass, as they provide early-season nectar for these skippers. Duskywings also bask on bare dirt and gravel areas.

Crownvetch (host)

Silver-spotted Skipper
Epargyreus clarus

M · A · M · J · J · A · S · O · N

Description
The Silver-spotted Skipper is recognized by a large white blotch on the underside of the hindwing and a large gold spot on the underside of the forewing. These butterflies rarely rest with their wings open, making viewing the upper wing surface nearly impossible.

Season
Silver-spotted Skipper activity begins late spring and continues through summer.

Habitat
Look for Silver-spotted Skippers in open areas, including fields, gardens, and parks.

Black Locust blossom (Host)

Host Plant
Black Locust, *Robinia pseudoacacia*, and wisteria. Black Locust is a tree that grows to 30 feet, while wisteria is a naturalized exotic woody vine.

Attracting to Your Garden
Silver-spotted Skippers are highly attracted to milkweed. Milkweed in the garden with nearby Black Locust trees should yield good results.

Delaware Skipper
Anatrytone logan

| M | A | M | J | J | A | S | O | N |

Description
This skipper looks like so many of the other little orange skippers. Look on the upper wing surface for dark veins on an orange background with a relatively uniform dark submarginal band.

Season
Delawares fly during the heat of the summer.

Habitat
Look for this skipper in parks, fields, gardens, and woodland openings.

Host Plant
A variety of native grasses.

Grama Grass (Host)

Attracting to Your Garden
A strong supply of nectar sources, especially milkweed, will improve your chances of attracting skippers in general, and the Delaware Skipper in particular. A planting of native grasses (not lawn grasses) will increase your chances.

Little Glassywing
Pompeius verna

M A M J J A S O N

Description

The Little Glassywing is a small dark skipper. The upper surface is most distinctive with white spots on a dark background. Likely to be confused with the female Zabulon Skipper (next page), the two large white spots on the wing are separated by a very thin line in the Glassywing. The female Zabulon also has a frosted look on the undersides of the wings.

Season

Look for Glassywings during the heat of the summer.

Habitat

Look for Little Glassywing in gardens, fields, and woodland openings.

Host Plant

Purpletop Grass. This summer grass grows to 36 inches high.

Attracting to Your Garden

A strong supply of nectar sources, especially milkweed in combination with nearby plantings of Purpletop Grass should attract this skipper to your garden.

Zabulon Skipper
Poanes zabulon

| M | A | M | J | J | A | S | O | N |

Description

This skipper is sexually dimorphic, meaning males and females look considerably different. Females are dark above with white spots, while males are orange above with marginal dark bands and a dark bar toward the middle of the forewing. Also look for a "frosted" appearance on the underside of the female's hindwing.

Male

Female

Season

Late spring through fall.

Habitat

Zabulon Skippers frequent open areas like parks, gardens, and fields as well as wooded edges and wooded roads.

Host Plant

A variety of native grasses.

Attracting to Your Garden

A selection of native grasses and perching sites are key to attracting this species. Notice in both of the above pictures, the skipper is perching on grass leaves. To create perching sites, do not dead head all of the previous season's grass and perennial heads.

Least Skipper
Ancyloxyphz numitor

M   A   M   J   J   A   S   O   N

Description

This super-small skipper is recognized by the solid pale orange on the underside of the wings. They rarely open their wings, but when doing so, the upperside has pale dark margins on an orange background.

Season

Least Skipper flies late spring through autumn.

Habitat

Least Skippers prefer open areas like parks, gardens, and fields.

Host Plant

A variety of native grasses.

Attracting to Your Garden

Planting a variety of native grasses and having a relatively open garden area will attract Least Skippers to your butterfly garden.

Common Checkered Skipper
Pyrgus communis

| M | A | M | J | J | A | S | O | N |

Description
In the Midwest, the Common Checkered Skipper is one of the few black and white speckled butterflies that will be encountered. They are locally common, meaning they may be quite prevalent at one site and then completely absent just a few miles down the road.

Swamp Mallow (Host)

Season
Checkered Skippers fly late spring into autumn.

Habitat
Common Checkered Skippers utilize a variety of habitats, but mostly open fields, parks, and gardens, but do not be surprised to seem them in woodland openings and edges.

Host Plant
The mallow family.

Attracting to Your Garden
Several members of the mallow family. are weeds in our area. Low growing members of the sunflower family are especially attractive to Checkered Skippers along with a butterfly garden with a more open feel.

Hummingbird Clearwing Moth
Hemaris thysbe

| M | A | M | J | J | A | S | O | N |

Description
While this is not a butterfly, this moth is such a delightful visitor to the butterfly garden it had to be included. This moth is easily recognized by the green and red body and the hovering behavior it exhibits while nectaring.

Season
Hummingbird Moths are active throughout the butterfly season.

Habitat
Primarily wooded openings and edges.

Host Plant
This species utilizes a variety of hosts, including honeysuckle (*Lonicera sp.*), cherry and plum (*Prunus sp.*), and Hawthorn (*Crataegus sp.*).

Hawthorne (Host) in fall foliage

Attracting to Your Garden
The Clearwing Hummingbird Moth's primary nectar preferences are Woodland Phlox (*Phlox divaricata)* in the spring and bergamot (*Monarda sp.*) in the summer. Nectar plantings at wooded edges or openings will be especially helpful.

Snowberry Clearwing Moth
Hemaris diffinis

| M | A | M | J | J | A | S | O | N |

Description
The Snowberry Clearwing Moth is different from the Hummingbird Clearwing in having a black and yellow body, making it look more like a bumblebee at first glance. It is also about the size of a bumblebee.

Season
This moth is active April through August.

Habitat
Primarily wooded openings, edges, and fields with adequate nectar.

Host Plant
This species utilizes a variety of hosts, including honeysuckle (*Lonicera sp.*), Snowberry (*Symphoricarpos orbiculatus*), and Indian Hemp (*Apocynum sp.*).

Western Snowberry (S. oreophilus)

Attracting to Your Garden
Attracting this novelty to your garden is more a function of the availability of host plants than nectar plants. Start with planting Indian Hemp (a great nectar plant also) and Snowberry to get the life cycle started. Milkweed and bergamot will then bring these beauties into view.

5
Native Nectar

Red-banded Hairstreak

Chapter 5

Native Nectar

Virginia Bluebells

Mertensia virginica

Description
Virginia Bluebells have light blue tubular flowers, about an inch long. The plant grows to 18 inches tall.

Season
Bluebells provide nectar throughout most of the month of April.

Habitat
This plant is typically found in floodplain woods and woodland edges. It may need occasional watering in home landscapes during prolonged dry periods. Plant in partial shade.

Attraction
Virginia Bluebells will attract primarily larger butterflies due to the long length of the floral tube. Look for Eastern Tiger Swallowtails to repeatedly visit your Bluebells patch!

Eastern Tiger Swallowtail

Spring Beauty
Claytonia virginica

| M | A | M | J | J | A | S | O | N |

Description
Spring Beauty has white to pink flowers with semi-succulent leaves. This spring perennial grows to about six inches tall.

Season
This species provides nectar from late March to early May.

Habitat
Spring Beauty occupies a variety of habitats, from rich, wet woods to upland woods to even lawns. Plant in full sun to partial shade.

Spring Azure

Attraction
While Spring Beauty is not necessarily a butterfly magnet, Spring Azures (pictured left) will utilize this plant species as a nectar source in early spring.

Bluets
Houstonia caerulea

M   A   M   J   J   A   S   O   N

Description
Bluets grow in small clumps to four inches tall. The petals are pale purple with a yellow throat at the end of a long narrow tube. The leaves are all basal and typically go without notice.

Season
This species provides nectar from late March to early May.

Habitat
Bluets generally occupy drier sites, especially lawns and fields. Plant in full sun.

Hobomok Skipper

Attraction
Like Spring Beauty, Bluets are not necessarily a butterfly magnet, but they do provide Spring Azures and skippers an early-season nectar source when not much else is available.

Woodland Phlox
Phlox divaricata

| | | | | | | | | |
|M|A|M|J|J|A|S|O|N|

Description
Woodland Phlox is a perennial that stands about 12 inches tall. Flower color can vary from nearly white to pale purple or pink.

Season
This plant blooms throughout most of April into early May.

Habitat
In its native habitat, this plant grows along woodland edges as well as deep woods. For best results, plant in full to partial sun.

Attraction
Woodland Phlox primarily attracts

larger butterflies, specifically Eastern Tiger and Spicebush Swallowtails. While not a major butterfly magnet, Phlox does provide nectar during a period in which nectar availability can be sparse, especially for large butterflies. A mass planting of this beauty will have a stronger attraction.

Blackberry/Raspberry
Rubus sp.

| | | | | | | | | | |
|M|A|M|J|J|A|S|O|N|

Description

Berry canes are characterized by having three to five leaflets with spines and will stand about three feet tall. They can form large patches if permitted. Raspberry stems will have a powdery blush (pruinose), which blackberries lack. The white flowers typically have five petals and are about an inch across.

Season

Berries bloom late April through May.

Habitat

Look for berries along roadsides, woodland edges, fence rows, and along gas and power line cuts. Plant in full sun to partial shade.

Silver-spotted Skipper

Attraction

While berries are not a primary butterfly attractant, they are utilized by butterflies at a time when little other nectar is available. Of course, another benefit of incorporating berries into the butterfly garden is the delicious harvest of fruit you will reap in the summer!

Purple Milkweed
Asclepias purpurascens

Description

Purple Milkweed has pinkish-purple flowers in an umbel that is two to three inches across. This perennial will reach three feet in height. This is one of the broad-leaved milkweeds.

Season

This species provides nectar from late May through late June.

Habitat

In nature, Purple Milkweed is found primarily along roadsides and woodland edges. Plant in full sun to half-day sun.

Great Spangled Fritillary

Attraction

Purple Milkweed is the first of the summer-blooming milkweeds, and there is no better butterfly magnet than milkweed. Great Spangled Fritillaries are especially fond of this nectar source as evidenced in the picture to the left. Use this species in conjunction with Common Milkweed and Butterfly Weed to maintain a milkweed nectar source throughout the summer. **Milkweed is the host plant of the monarch.**

Common Milkweed
Asclepias syriaca

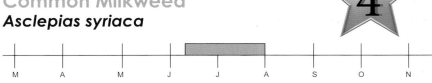

| M | A | M | J | J | A | S | O | N |

Description
Common Milkweed has pinkish-purple flowers in an umbel that is two to three inches across. This perennial will reach three to four feet in height. This is another of the broad-leaved milkweeds.

Season
This species provides nectar from mid-June through late July.

Habitat
In nature, Common Milkweed is found primarily along roadsides and in open fields. Plant in full sun.

Attraction
Common Milkweed follows directly behind the flowering period of Purple

Black Swallowtail

Milkweed. Common Milkweed attracts large butterflies like swallowtails and fritillaries but also attracts the smaller skippers, and for that reason is perhaps one of the most versatile of our native butterfly plants. Common Milkweed will prefer more open and sunny garden areas. **Milkweed is the host plant of the monarch.**

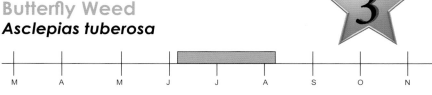

| M | A | M | J | J | A | S | O | N |

Description

Butterfly Weed has yellow to orange flowers in flat-topped inflorescences. This perennial will reach 18 inches in height. This is the only milkweed with alternate leaf arrangement, rather than the usual opposite arrangement of milkweeds.

Season

Butterfly Weed rounds out the milkweed trifecta, blooming late June through mid-August.

Habitat

Butterfly Weed prefers open fields and roadsides. Plant in full sun.

Eastern Tiger Swallowtail with Great Spangled Fritillary

Attraction

By planting all three milkweeds, Purple, Showy, and Butterfly Weed, you will have constant butterfly magnets and incredible color the entire summer. The nectar of Butterfly Weed is a strong attractant for fritillaries, hairstreaks, swallowtails, and monarchs. **Milkweed is the host plant of the monarch.**

Swamp Milkweed
Asclepias incarnata

8

| | | | | | | | | |
|M|A|M|J|J|A|S|O|N|

Description

Swamp Milkweed grows to five feet tall and has pink flowers. The leaves of this milkweed are narrower compared to other Midwestern milkweeds.

Season

Swamp Milkweed blooms throughout July.

Habitat

This species very much likes to have its feet wet. Look for it in consistently wet roadside ditches and wetland edges. Plant in full sun.

Attraction

Swamp Milkweed, while not as strong of an attractant as the other milkweeds, is still a valuable part of any butterfly garden. **Milkweed is the host plant of the monarch.**

Snowberry Clearwing Moth

Mountain Mint
Pycnanthemum sp.

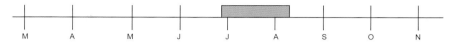

M	A	M	J	J	A	S	O	N

Description
Mountain Mint will catch your attention with large clusters of white flowers dotted with purple. The leaves are quite narrow. This plant grows to 24 inches high and prefers full sun. There are several different species of *Pycnanthemum*.

Season
Mountain Mint blooms throughout July and into August.

Habitat
Look for Mountain Mint in open fields and along woodland edges. Plant in full sun.

Pearl Crescent

Attraction
Mountain Mint is especially attractive to smaller butterflies like crescents, hairstreaks, and skippers.

Indian Hemp
Apocynum cannabinum

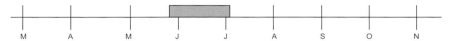

M   A   M   J   J   A   S   O   N

Description
Indian Hemp grows to three to four feet in height and has terminal clusters of small white flowers. This plant is closely related to the milkweeds, and shares their strong butterfly attraction and their opposite leaf arrangement.

Banded Hairstreak

Season
Indian Hemp blooms from late May through June.

Habitat
This species grows along roadsides and in open fields. Plant in full sun.

Great Spangled Fritillary

Attraction
Indian Hemp is a great attractor for smaller butterflies like skippers and hairstreaks. Fritillaries will also visit this species if milkweed is not readily available. Indian Hemp can be colonial, meaning it will form large patches if permitted. It would be recommended to give Indian Hemp its own bed in the garden to control it more easily.

Wild Basil
Satureja vulgaris

M   A   M   J   J   A   S   O   N

Description
Wild Basil is another summer blooming member of the mint family of plants. This plant stands up to 12 inches tall, with clusters of pink tubular flowers spread along the upper half of the stem. The aromatic foliage gives this plant away as a mint.

Season
Look for Wild Basil to bloom the back half of June and front half of July.

Habitat
Wild Basil grows in open fields and along woodland edges. Plant in full sun to partial shade.

Gray Hairstreak

Attraction
Wild Basil will attract smaller butterflies, especially skippers, sulphurs, hairstreaks, and whites.

Wild Bergamot
Monarda fistulosa

5

| M | A | M | J | J | A | S | O | N |

Description
Wild Bergamot has the characteristic square stem of the mint family with aromatic foliage. The plants are up to 24 inches tall with clusters of slender, tubular, pink to pale purple flowers.

Season
Look for Wild Bergamot to bloom in July and August.

Habitat
Monarda grows along woodland edges, roadsides, and gas and power line cuts. Plant in full sun to partial shade.

Clearwing Hummingbird Moth

Attraction
Wild Bergamot attracts a wide variety of butterflies, from whites and sulphurs to fritillaries and swallowtails and even hummingbird moths. Consider this plant a "must have" for your summer butterfly garden, second only to milkweed for its attractive potential!

Purple Coneflower
Echinacea purpurea

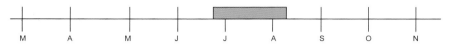

M   A   M   J   J   A   S   O   N

Description

Purple Coneflower has purple ray flowers with a red-orange disk. Each flower head can be as wide as four inches. The plants stand 24 inches high.

Season

Look for Purple Coneflower to bloom in the heat of summer, from late June to early August.

Habitat

This perennial is a prairie plant in its native condition. It is widely used in the landscaping trade and should be readily available at any garden center.

Monarch

Attraction

Purple Coneflower attracts a wide range of butterfly species, from small skippers to large swallowtails. Mass plantings are recommended as individual plants or widely scattered plants will be overlooked by butterflies in favor of more profuse blooming neighboring plants.

Blazing Star
Liatris squarrosa

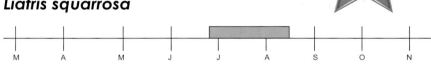

M | A | M | J | J | A | S | O | N

Description
This Liatris is noticeably different from the Liatris typically available at garden centers. This Liatris has a much shorter flower spike with much longer individual flowers.

Season
Look for Blazing Star in the heat of the summer, and essentially the same season as Purple Coneflower, late June through early August.

Habitat
In its native condition, this plant is a prairie perennial. Because of its unique form and attractiveness, this species is now readily available in the nursery trade.

Giant Swallowtail

Attraction
As a butterfly magnet, this plant can easily share the same stage with milkweed and Joe Pye, as evidenced by the Giant Swallowtail nectaring in the photo on the left. A mass planting of this species will attract butterflies for miles around! All of the Liatrises are great butterfly plants, but L. squarrosa is perhaps the best of the best!

Wingstem
Verbesinia alternifolia

| | | | | | | | | |
|M|A|M|J|J|A|S|O|N|

Description
Wingstem is a member of the sunflower family, with very loose flower heads at the end of stem branches. Ray and disk flowers are yellow. As the common name implies, leafy wings extend down the stem. Plants grow to four feet tall.

Season
Look for Wingstem to bloom the end of July through mid-September.

Habitat
Wingstem naturally grows in woodland openings and edges. Plant in full sun to partial shade.

Attraction
Wingstem will attract smaller butterflies, especially skippers. **Wingstem is the host plant of the Silvery Checkerspot.**

Joe Pye Weed
Eupatorium sp.

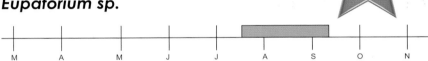

| | | | | | | | | |
|M|A|M|J|J|A|S|O|N|

Description

Joe Pye Weed has large pink flower clusters at the end of the enormously tall stems. It is easily recognized by the whorl of several leaves at each node. Joe Pye Weed grows to six feet tall.

Season

Look for Joe Pye Weed blooming during August.

Habitat

Joe Pye Weed grows naturally at the edges of wet meadows and woodland edges. Plant in partial shade.

Attraction

Joe Pye Weed will attract a variety of small and large butterflies, including skippers, fritillaries, and swallowtails.

Monarch

Sunflower
Helianthus sp.

M A M J J A S O N

Description

There are several different *Helianthus* species that grow thoughout the Midwest. *Helianthus decapetalus* is among the strongest attractants of the sunflowers. Wild sunflowers generally stand three to four feet high. Another group of plants that looks very similar and also has butterfly attracting abilities is the genus *Silphium*, which includes Prairie Dock and Cup Plant.

Season

Look for our native sunflowers in late summer, largely from late July to early September.

Habitat

Most of the sunflower species prefer forest openings in full sun. Helianthus microcephalus prefers more shaded habitats.

Eastern Tiger Swallowtail

Attraction

The sunflowers are strong attractants for larger butterfly species like swallowtails and monarchs. Sunflowers are a strong butterfly plant for areas where Joe Pye Weed is not available.

Mistflower
Eupatorium coelestinum

| | | | | | | | | | |
|M|A|M|J|J|A|S|O|N|

Description
Mistflower stands about 12 inches tall, topped by blue, aster-like flowers.

Season
Mistflower is a late season flower, blooming from mid-August through September.

Habitat
Mistflower normally grows in woodland openings and powerline/gasline cuts. Full sun would be best for this low-growing accent plant.

Attraction
Unfortunately for Mistflower, it blooms during the same season as some of the most powerful butterfly attractants. So, in nature, Mistflower is not as visited as the nearby Joe Pyes and Ironweeds, but a good butterfly plant nonetheless. Pearl Crescents, Silvery Checkerspots, and other smaller butterfly species will still visit Mistflower.

Pearl Crescent

Thistle
Cirsium sp.

M	A	M	J	J	A	S	O	N

Description

Thistles are known for their prickly spines throughout the plant, topped by a large pink flower head. There are several native thistles in our area, and most grow four to six feet tall. Avoid Canadian Thistle as it is highly invasive. This thistle has small flower heads, barely one-half inch across. While thistle has the reputation of being a "weed," most are native to our area, and only Canadian Thistle will take over a site. And, butterflies love them!

Season

Thistles bloom late summer, from August into September.

Habitat

In nature, thistles grow in fields and wooded edges. Plant in full sun to half-day sun.

Clearwing Hummingbird Moth

Attraction

Thistles attract the whole range of butterflies, from small skippers to large swallowtails. It is even a favorite of hummingbird moths! **Thistle is the host plant of the Painted Lady.**

Buttonbush
Cephalanthus occidentalis

| M | A | M | J | J | A | S | O | N |

Description
Buttonbush can become a large shrub to 15 feet, with dark green leaves in whorls of three. The flower head is one inch in diameter covered with white tubular flowers. Habitat is key to identification of this species, as Buttonbush is one of the few shrubs that grow in swampy conditions.

Season
Buttonbush blooms mid- to late-summer.

Habitat
In nature, this plant grows in swampy conditions. It can be grown in the home landscape, but be prepared to give it extra water to maintain full vigor. Plant in full sun to half-day sun.

Spicebush Swallowtail

Attraction
Swallowtails are primarily the group of butterflies attracted to Buttonbush.

Ironweed
Vernonia altissima

| M | A | M | J | J | A | S | O | N |

Description
Ironweed is another member of the sunflower family. The bright purple flowers sit atop six-foot- tall stems.

Season
Ironweed is a late summer bloomer, starting late July and continuing to mid-September.

Habitat
Much like Joe Pye Weed, Ironweed prefers moist forest openings and woodland edges. Plant in full sun to half-day sun.

Zabulon Skipper

Attraction
Ironweed will attract butterflies of all shapes and sizes, but especially look for skippers to visit these beautiful purple flowers.

Goldenrod
Solidago sp.

| M | A | M | J | J | A | S | O | N |

Description
There are about fifteen different species of goldenrod native to the Midwest. All have clusters of small yellow flowers. Most stand 18 to 30 inches high.

Season
Goldenrods begin blooming midsummer; however, it is the later blooming species that seem to have the most appeal to butterflies. Look for it in September and even into October in mild autumns. *Solidago canadensis*, *S. erecta*, and *S. gigantea* are the more common of the late season goldenrods.

Habitat
Goldenrod in its natural condition is found in fields and woodland openings and edges. Plant in full sun to half-day sun.

Eastern Tiger Swallowtail

Attraction
While goldenrod frequently appeals to smaller butterflies, even large butterflies like this Tiger Swallowtail are enticed by its nectar.

Aster
Aster sp.

M | A | M | J | J | A | S | O | N

Description

There are many different species of asters native to the Midwest, occupying a variety of habitats. Aster in general is an excellent nectar source for butterflies. Most have purple or white ray flowers with yellow disk flowers. Most stand 18 to 24 inches high.

Season

Aster is a late-season bloomer. Look for asters in September and October and perhaps longer with favorable weather conditions.

Habitat

Asters occupy a variety of habitats, including woodland edges and openings, fields, and swampy areas. Plant in full sun to partial shade.

Gulf Fritillary

Attraction

Sulphurs and whites are especially attracted to asters, but even this Gulf Fritillary could not resist its charms. **Aster is the host plant of the Pearl Crescent.**

6
Gardener's Guide to
Host Plants

Monarch

TREES

Common Name	Scientific Name	Height
American Elm	Ulmus americana	100 feet
Black Cherry	Prunus serotina	90 feet
Black Locust	Robinia pseudoacacia	30 feet
Eastern Cottonwood (Caution: Roots invade plumbing)	Populus deltoides	100 feet
Eastern Red Cedar	Juniperus virginiana	15 feet
Flowering Dogwood	Cornus florida	30 feet
Hackberry	Celtis occidentalis	60 feet
Hickory	Carya sp.	100 feet

Chapter 6

Gardener's Guide to Host Plants

Sun/Shade	Flower Color	Fall Color	Associated Butterfly
Sun/Shade	NA	Yellow	Eastern Comma Question Mark
Sun/Shade	White	Yellow	Tiger Swallowtail, Coral Hairstreak, Spring Azure
Sun	White	Yellow	Silver-spotted Skipper
Sun	NA	Yellow	Dreamy Duskywing Mourning Cloak Red-spotted Purple
Sun	NA	Evergreen	Juniper Hairstreak
Sun	White	Red	Spring/Summer Azure
Sun/Shade	NA	Yellow	Snout Hackberry (or Tawny) Emperor
Sun/Shade	NA	Yellow	Banded Hairstreak Hickory Hairstreak

TREES

Common Name	Scientific Name	Height
Oak	Quercus sp. (multiple species of oaks)	60-90 feet
Pawpaw	Asimina triloba	20 feet
Redbud	Cercis canadensis	20 feet
Sassafras	Sassafras albidum	40 feet
Slippery Elm	Ulmus rubra	100 feet
Tulip Tree	Liriodendron tulipifera	100 feet
Wild Plum	Prunus americana	30 feet
Willow	Salix sp.	20-60 feet
Yellow Birch	Betula allegheniensis	90 feet

Sun/Shade	Flower Color	Fall Color	Associated Butterfly
Sun/Shade	NA	Yellow/Red	Banded Hairstreak, Edward's Hairstreak, Oak Hairstreak, White M Hairstreak, Juvenal's Duskywing, Horace's Duskywing, Sleepy Duskywing
Partial Shade/ Full Shade	Red	Yellow	Zebra Swallowtail
Sun	Pink	Yellow	Henry's Elfin
Sun	Yellow	Yellow	Spicebush Swallowtail
Sun/Shade	NA	Yellow	Eastern Comma Question Mark
Sun	Yellow/Orange	Yellow	Tiger Swallowtail
Sun/Shade	White	Yellow	Coral Hairstreak
Sun	NA	Yellow	Dreamy Duskywing Mourning Cloak Red-spotted Purple Viceroy Acadian Hairstreak
Sun/Shade	NA	Yellow	Early Hairstreak

SHRUBS

Common Name	Scientific Name	Height
Arrowwood	Viburnum dentatum	6 feet
Black Haw	Viburnum prunifolium	6 feet
Dogwood (several shrubby species)	Cornus sp.	6-15 feet
Low-bush Blueberry	Vaccinium angustifolium	4 feet
Spicebush	Lindera benzoin	6 feet
Sumac (several species; shrubby to small trees)	Rhus sp.	15 feet
Willow	Salix sp.	20-60 feet

Sun/Shade	Flower Color	Fall Color	Associated Butterfly
Shade	White	Yellow	Spring Azure Baltimore Checkerspot
Shade	White	Yellow	Spring Azure Baltimore Checkerspot
Sun/Shade	White	Red	Spring/Summer Azure
Sun	Cream	Red	Brown Elfin Henry's Elfin Striped Hairstreak Spring Azure
Shade	Yellow	Yellow	Spicebush Swallowtail
Sun	Yellow	Red	Red-banded Hairstreak
Sun	NA	Yellow	Dreamy Duskywing Mourning Cloak Red-spotted Purple Viceroy Acadian Hairstreak

WILDFLOWERS

Common Name	Scientific Name	Height
Aster	Aster sp.	24 inches
Black Cohosh	Cimicifuga racemosa	3 feet
Carrot Family	Apiaceae	Variable
Columbine	Aquilegia canadensis	12 inches
Frogfruit	Phyla lanceolata	Groundcover
Goat's Beard	Aruncus dioicus	5 feet
Mallow Family	Malvaceae	2-6 feet
Milkweed	Asclepias sp.	12-48 inches
Monkeyflower	Mimulus ringens	24 inches

Sun/Shade	Flower Color	Bloom/Time	Associated Butterfly
Sun	White, purple	September, October	Pearl Crescent Silvery Checkerspot
Shade	White	June	Spring Azure Appalachian Azure
Variable	Most are white, yellow	Variable	Black Swallowtail
Shade	Red	April, May	Columbine Duskywing
Sun/Shade	Pink	June-August	Buckeye
Shade	White	May-June	Dusky Azure
Sun	White, Pink, Red	June-August	Common Checkered Skipper Gray Hairstreak
Sun (most species)	White, pink, red, purple, orange	May-August	Monarch
Sun (& wet)	Purple	July	Buckeye

WILDFLOWERS

Common Name	Scientific Name	Height
Rock Cress	Arabis sp.	18 inches
Senna	Senna hebecarpa	6 feet
Sunflower	Helianthus sp.	4-5 feet
Thistle	Cirsium sp.	4-6 feet
Toothwort	Cardamine sp.	6-12 inches
Turtlehead	Chelone glabra	24 inches
Violets	Viola sp.	Groundcover
Virginia Snakeroot	Aristolochia serpentaria	12 inches

Sun/Shade	Flower Color	Bloom/Time	Associated Butterfly
Shade	Purple	May	Falcate Orangetip Olympia Marble West Virginia White
Sun	Yellow	July, August	Cloudless Sulphur, Little Yellow, Sleepy Orange
Sun/Shade	Yellow	July, August	Silvery Checkerspot
Sun/Partial Shade	Pink	August, September	Painted Lady
Shade	White	April, May	Cabbage White West Virginia White Checkered White
Shade	White	July, August	Baltimore Checkerspot
Shade	White, Yellow, Purple	April, May	Great Spangled Fritillary Meadow Fritillary Aphrodite Fritillary Variegated Fritillary Regal Fritillary Diana Fritillary
Shade	Red	May, June	Pipevine Swallowtail

GRASSES

Common Name	Scientific Name	Height
Big Bluestem	Andropogon geradii	8 feet
Giant Cane	Arundinaria gigantean	10 feet
Grass Family	Poaceae	Variable
Little Bluestem	Schizachyrium scoparius	4 feet

Sun/Shade	Flower Color	Bloom/Time	Associated Butterfly
Sun	NA	NA	Crossline Skipper
Sun/Shade	NA	NA	Creole Pearly-eye Southern Pearly-eye
Variable	NA	NA	Appalachian Brown Carolina Satyr Common Wood Nymph Crossline Skipper Fiery Skipper Gemmed Satyr Indian Skipper Least Skipper Leonard's Skipper Little Wood Satyr Northern Pearly-eye Pepper and Salt Skipper Clouded Skipper Bell's Roadside Skipper Ottoe Skipper Poweshiek Skipperling
Sun	NA	NA	Cobweb Skipper Swarthy Skipper Common Roadside Skipper

GRASSES

Common Name	Scientific Name	Height
Panic Grass	Panicum sp.	24 inches
Purpletop Grass	Tridens flavus	4 feet
Rice Cutgrass	Leersia oryzoides	4 feet

Sun/Shade	Flower Color	Bloom/Time	Associated Butterfly
Sun/Shade	NA	NA	Hobomok Skipper Northern Broken Dash
Sun	NA	NA	Little Glassywing
Sun	NA	NA	Least Skipper

7
Sources for Native Plants

Aphrodite Fritillary

Index

Notes

Notes

Notes

Notes

Notes

Notes

Notes

Notes

Notes

Notes

Notes